First Facts®

FACT FILES

U.S. LANDFORMS

What You Need to Know

by LINDA CROTTA BRENNAN

CAPSTONE PRESS
a capstone imprint

First Facts are published by Capstone Press,
1710 Roe Crest Drive, North Mankato, Minnesota 56003
www.mycapstone.com

Library of Congress Cataloging-in-Publication Data
Library of Congress Cataloging-in-Publication data is available on the Library of Congress website.
ISBN 978-1-5157-8112-7 (library binding)
ISBN 978-1-5157-8125-7 (paperback)
ISBN 978-1-5157-8132-5 (eBook PDF)

Editorial Credits
Mandy Robbins, editor; Jenny Bergstrom, designer; Kelly Garvin, media researcher; Laura Manthe, production specialist

Photo Credits
Science Source: Gary Hincks, 7 (top insets), Planet Observer, 14; Shutterstock: Bardocz Peter, 17, Chawalit Siwaborwornwattana, 24, Dan Thornberg, cover (top left), 1, Doug Meek, 13, ESCLASANS, cover (bottom right), Felix Nendzig, cover (top right), Galyna Andrushko, cover (bottom left), Greg Brave, 21, Jeffrey M. Frank, 9, Jess Kraft, 8, Jim Guy, 17 (top middle), Kenneth Keifer, 15, Kevin Eaves, 3, Lucky-photographer, backcover, mapichai, 19, Peter Kunasz, 11, Ricardo Reitmeyer, 7, robert cicchetti, 22, sergei kochetov, 5, Shoriful Chowdhury, 17 (tr), snapgalleria, 9 (top inset), Zack Frank, 16, 17 (tl)

Printed in the United States 5756

Table of Contents

Shaping the Earth

Imagine you're building a sandcastle. Your fingers shape the sand into different forms. Like your fingers, natural forces shape Earth into different landforms.

A landform is part of Earth's surface. Mountains and valleys are examples of landforms. ***Volcanoes*** and ***glaciers*** cause some of the forces that shape landforms.

volcano—an opening in the earth's surface that sometimes sends out hot lava, steam, and ash
glacier—a huge moving body of ice that flows down a mountain slope or across a polar region

Flatlands

Plains are flatlands. They are the most common landform on Earth. ***Coastal plains*** line the eastern United States. The Great Plains are in the middle of the United States. Long ago, a shallow sea covered these plains. Over millions of years, rock and soil settled. The sea dried up. Flatlands remained.

coastal plain—a large area of low, flat land near the ocean that was once covered by water

NORTH AMERICA

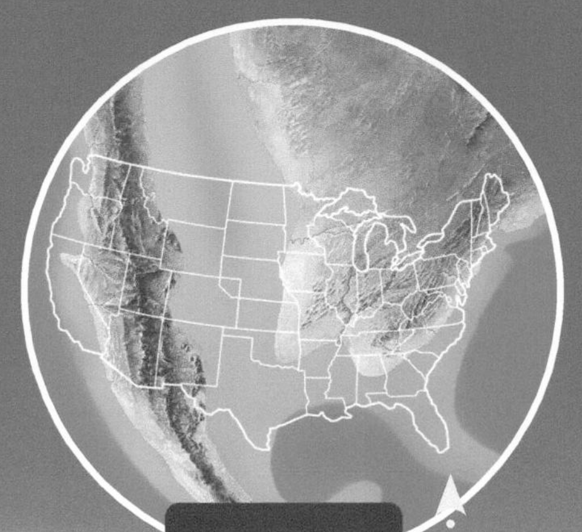

105 million years ago

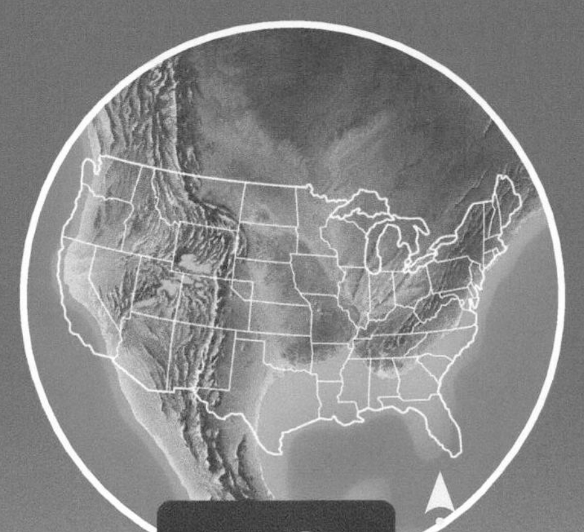

60 million years ago

40 million years ago

Highlands

Earth's top layer is broken into ***plates***. When the plates meet, mountains, hills, and ***plateaus*** can form. Hills are high. Mountains are even higher. They have steep sides and narrow tops. Mountains tower above their surroundings. A plateau is a highland with a flat top.

FACT

Another name for plateaus is tablelands. They are high but flat, like a table.

BLACK HILLS, SOUTH DAKOTA

plate—a large sheet of rock that is a piece of Earth's crust
plateau—an area of high, flat land

MOUNTAINS
HILLS
PLATEAUS

The Appalachian Mountains are on the east side of North America. Almost 500 million years ago, two plates hit each other. They pushed these mountains up.

The Rocky Mountains lie on the west side of North America. They were formed by one plate sliding under another plate.

ROCKY MOUNTAINS

Deep Lands

A valley is a low area surrounded by highlands. A ***canyon*** is a narrow, rocky valley with steep sides. A fast-flowing river usually forms a canyon. Over time, the river wears away the land. It carves out the canyon. The Colorado River carved out the Grand Canyon.

FACT

The Grand Canyon is so big you can see it from space.

canyon—a deep, narrow area with steep sides; a canyon often has a stream or a river running through it

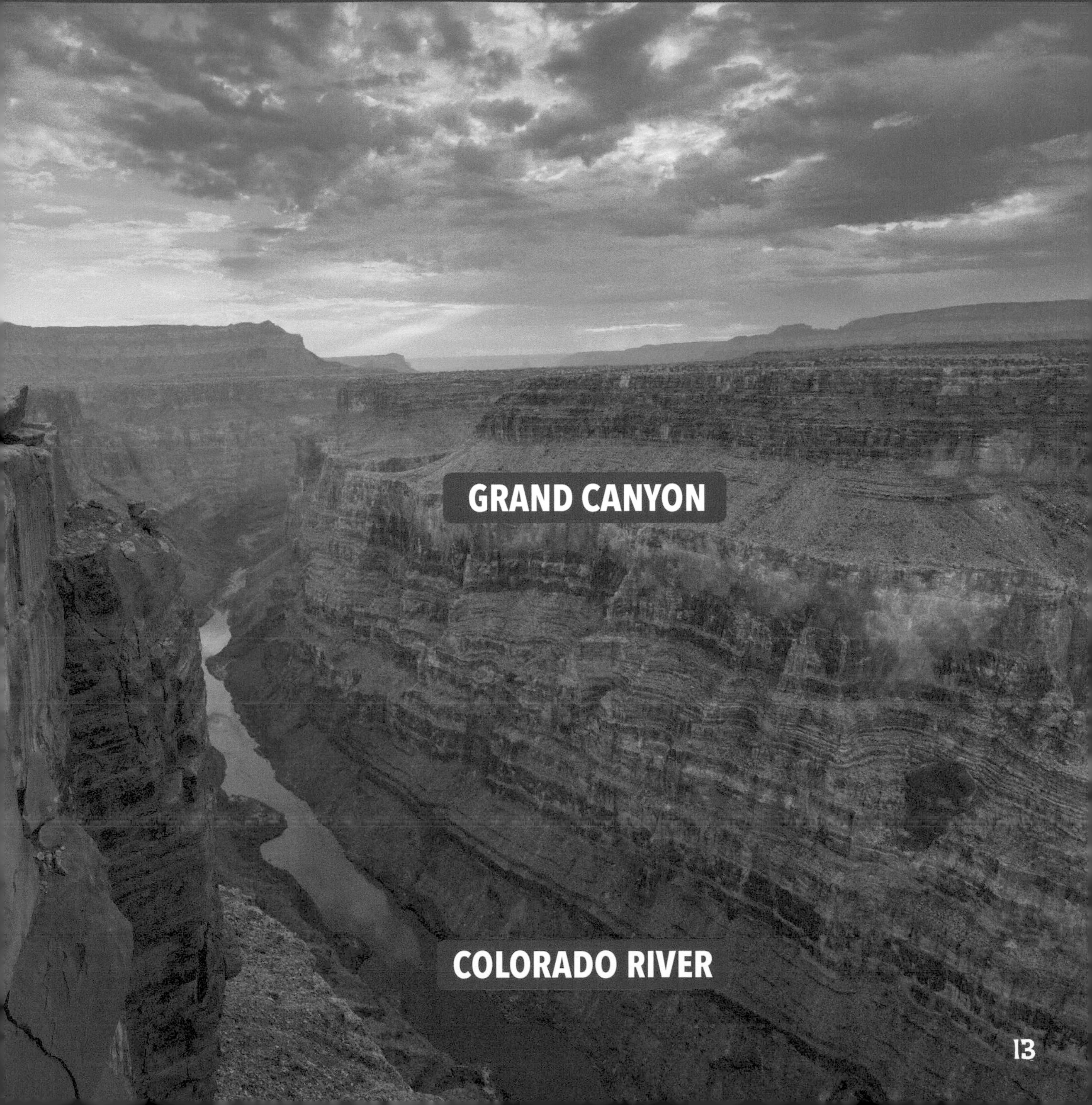

GRAND CANYON

COLORADO RIVER

Water

Lakes are bodies of water surrounded by land. The Great Lakes are five huge, connected lakes. They lie along the northern edge of the United States. The Great Lakes were formed during the last ***ice age***. Giant glaciers dug hollows into the earth. Then the temperature warmed, and the glaciers melted. Water filled the hollows.

ice age—a period of time when much of Earth was covered in ice; the last ice age ended about 11,500 years ago

LAKE MICHIGAN

A river is a large body of flowing water. The Mississippi River runs through the center of the United States. More water flows through it than any other river in North America.

When a river drops over a cliff, it forms a ***waterfall***. Niagara Falls is a famous waterfall. It is found in the United States and Canada.

The Rio Grande is a large river separating the United States from Mexico.

waterfall—a place where river water falls from a high place to a lower place

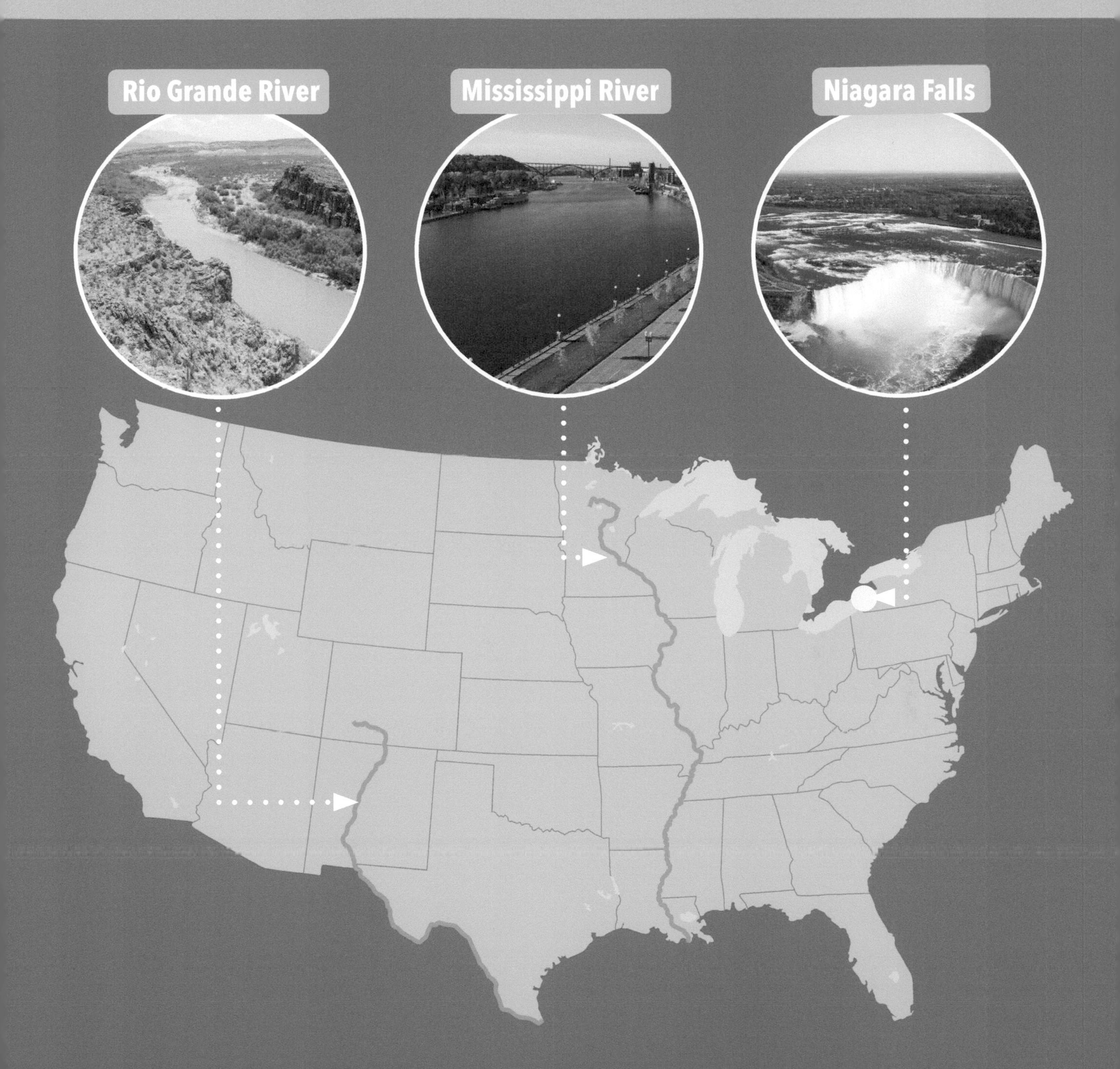
Rio Grande River
Mississippi River
Niagara Falls

Where Land Meets Water

An island is land surrounded by water. The state of Hawaii is a ***chain*** of 132 islands. Volcanoes in the Pacific Ocean formed Hawaii's islands. Each time a volcano erupted, it left behind a layer of hardened ***lava***. The layers stacked tall enough to rise above the sea's surface.

chain—a series of connected things
lava—the hot, liquid rock that pours out of a volcano when it erupts

A peninsula is land surrounded by water on three sides. It is connected to a larger landmass on one side. The state of Florida is a peninsula.

Landforms are all around us. Volcanoes formed some. Others were scraped out by glaciers or carved by rivers. What landforms are near you?

Glossary

canyon (KAN-yuhn)—a deep, narrow area with steep sides; a canyon often has a stream or a river running through it

chain (CHAYN)—a series of connected things

coastal plain (KOHS-tuhl PLAYN)—a large area of low, flat land near the ocean that was once covered by water

glacier (GLAY-shur)—a huge moving body of ice that flows down a mountain slope or across a polar region

ice age (EYESS AYJ)—a period of time when much of Earth was covered in ice; the last ice age ended about 11,500 years ago

lava (LAH-vuh)—the hot, liquid rock that pours out of a volcano when it erupts

plate (PLAYT)—a large sheet of rock that is a piece of Earth's crust

plateau (pla-TOH)—an area of high, flat land

volcano (vol-KAY-noh)—an opening in the earth's surface that sometimes sends out hot lava, steam, and ash

waterfall (WAH-tur-fahl)—a place where river water falls from a high place to a lower place

Read More

Dee, Willa. *Erosion and Weathering.* Rocks: The Hard Facts. New York: PowerKids Press, 2014.

Oxlade, Chris. *Mountains.* Learning About Landforms. North Mankato, Minn.: Capstone Publishing, 2014.

Spilsbury, Louise. *What Is a Landform?* Let's Find Out: Earth Science. New York: Rosen Publishing, 2014.

Internet Sites

Use FactHound find Internet sites related to this book.

Visit *www.facthound.com*

Just type in 9781515781127

Check out projects, games and lots more at
www.capstonekids.com

Critical Thinking Questions

1. Over millions of years, wind and rain wear away mountains bit by bit. The Rocky Mountains are much taller than the Appalachian Mountains. Which mountains do you think are older? Why?
2. Would you rather live near a volcano or a glacier? Why?
3. What landforms are near your home? How do you think they'll look in 100 million years?

Index